Children's Illustrators

Brian Selznick

Sheila Griffin Llanas
ABDO Publishing Company

visit us at
www.abdopublishing.com

Published by ABDO Publishing Company, PO Box 398166, Minneapolis, MN 55439. Copyright © 2012 by Abdo Consulting Group, Inc. International copyrights reserved in all countries. No part of this book may be reproduced in any form without written permission from the publisher. The Checkerboard Library™ is a trademark and logo of ABDO Publishing Company.

Printed in the United States of America, North Mankato, Minnesota.
102011
012012

Cover Photo: Corbis
Interior Photos: Alamy pp. 14–15; AP Images pp. 9, 13; Jamey Mazzie / courtesy Scholastic Inc. p. 5;
    Sara Krulwich / The New York Times / Redux p. 7
    Reprinted with the permission of Atheneum Books for Young Readers, an imprint of Simon & Schuster Children's Publishing Division from *The Houdini Box* written and illustrated by Brian Selznick. Copyright © 1991, 2008 Brian Selznick. p. 11
    From *The Invention of Hugo Cabret* by Brian Selznick. Scholastic Inc. / Scholastic Press. Copyright © 2007 by Brian Selznick. Reprinted by permission. pp. 16, 17, 19
    From *Wonderstruck* by Brian Selznick. Scholastic Inc. / Scholastic Press. Copyright © 2011 by Brian Selznick. Used by permission. pp. 20, 21

Series Coordinator: BreAnn Rumsch / Editors: Megan M. Gunderson, BreAnn Rumsch
Art Direction: Neil Klinepier

Library of Congress Cataloging-in-Publication Data

Llanas, Sheila Griffin, 1958-
  Brian Selznick / Sheila Griffin Llanas.
    p. cm. -- (Children's illustrators)
  Includes index.
  ISBN 978-1-61783-248-2
  1. Selznick, Brian--Juvenile literature. 2. Illustrators--United States--Biography--Juvenile literature. I. Selznick, Brian. II. Title.
  NC975.5.S43L59 2012
  741.6'42--dc23
  [B]
                        2011027841

CONTENTS

LIFELONG ARTIST

Brian Selznick has been an artist since he was a little boy. He grew up drawing, painting, and sculpting. But he never thought he would write and illustrate children's books. It wasn't until after college that he knew this was the work he was meant to do.

Some of Selznick's books are based on his childhood interests. He loved monster movies, magicians, science fiction, and toys. As a boy, Selznick played with disguises. Then as an adult, he wrote and illustrated *The Boy of a Thousand Faces*.

Young Selznick was also inspired when he saw Georges Méliès's 1902 film *A Trip to the Moon*. In 2007, he published an award-winning book about that movie. It is called *The Invention of Hugo Cabret*.

Selznick has created numerous books for children and young people. He has had the great skill and the good fortune to turn his wonderful talents and ideas into an exciting career.

Selznick often looks to his own childhood to inspire his books.

WORLD OF WONDER

Brian Selznick was born on July 14, 1966. He grew up in East Brunswick, New Jersey, with a brother and a sister. Brian's parents are Lynn and Roger Selznick. Brian's father had dreamed of being an **archaeologist**. But he ended up being an **accountant**. He worked hard to give his children a chance to follow their dreams.

From a young age, Brian loved to read. One of his favorites was the picture book *Fortunately* by Remy Charlip. He also loved *The Borrowers* by Mary Norton. Brian thought this story about little people was true. So, he made tiny furniture for the Borrowers he thought were living in his own room.

Brian was an imaginative boy who made art all the time. He built a house for his toy trolls. When Brian's dog ate one of his troll's arms, Brian made a new arm out of clay. In his backyard woods, Brian built "G.I. Joe Island" with fortresses and roads.

Today, Brian's apartment is full of fun reminders from his childhood.

Movies also captured Brian's imagination. He loved *The Wizard of Oz* and *King Kong* and was obsessed with *Star Wars*. He also craved movies about monsters, insects, and werewolves. Brian loved to watch them in his mom and dad's bedroom. During scary parts, he hid behind their bed!

An Artist's Education

Brian attended public schools in East Brunswick. In fifth grade, he studied art with a teacher named Eileen Sutton. Brian continued his lessons with her until twelfth grade. Ms. Sutton taught Brian a lot about drawing and painting.

In high school, Brian's friends told him he should illustrate children's books. But Brian did not like that idea. His grandfather's cousin, David O. Selznick, was a famous movie producer. So, Brian thought he would one day work in film or theater.

After high school, Brian studied illustration at the Rhode Island School of Design (RISD) in Providence. For one assignment, Brian had to create something about magician and escape artist Harry Houdini. He made a folding sculpture of glass panels with pictures on them. Brian thought working on this project was a lot of fun. So, he even added a story about a boy who gets to meet Houdini.

When Brian graduated from RISD in 1988, he wanted to study **set** design. So he applied to the Yale School of Drama at Yale University in New Haven, Connecticut. But, he did not get in.

Brian felt unsure about what to do with his life. So, he traveled to Europe. He carried a notebook with him for drawing pictures and writing stories. That's when Brian realized he wanted to illustrate children's books after all.

Rhode Island School of Design

WORKING AT EEYORE'S

In 1989, Selznick moved to New York City, New York. He applied for a job at a bookstore called Eeyore's Books for Children. The job required a strong knowledge of children's literature. Selznick had studied art, but he knew nothing about children's books. So, he was not hired.

The manager, Steve Geck, told Selznick to read some children's books and come back. Geck did not think he would see Selznick again. But Selznick took his advice. When Selznick returned, he got the job!

At Eeyore's, Selznick learned all he could about children's books. Eeyore's carried more than 20,000 different books. Geck let Selznick take books home to read. Every evening, Selznick read 15 to 20 new books.

Selznick was amazed by all the wonderful stories he read. Feeling inspired, he showed his boss the Houdini story he had worked on in college. Selznick had added detailed pencil drawings to accompany the words.

Geck was impressed and showed the **manuscript** to an editor at Random House named Anne Schwartz. She published *The Houdini Box* in 1991. Selznick had his first book! It even won the 1993 Texas Bluebonnet and Rhode Island Children's Book awards.

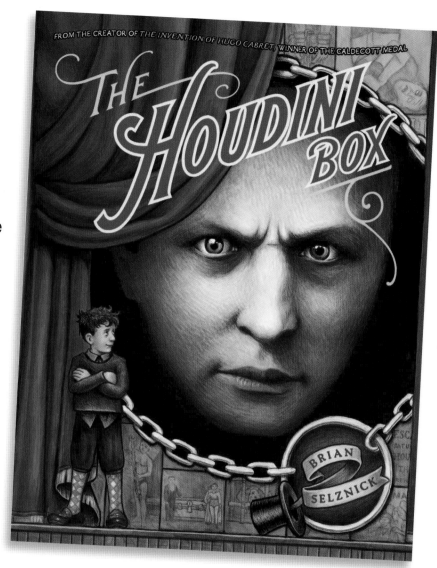

The Start of a Career

Selznick loved working at Eeyore's. He learned much about children's books, and he met many people in the publishing business. But to create more books of his own, Selznick needed more time to draw and paint. So after three years, he decided to leave the bookstore.

Selznick's editor, Laura Geringer, soon asked him to illustrate *Doll Face Has a Party*. The story was by Pam Conrad, one of Selznick's favorite children's authors! He was thrilled to have the job.

During the project, Selznick learned that the writer and the artist can have different ideas for a picture book. Conrad had imagined Doll Face as very quiet. But Selznick had painted her like a movie star! Luckily, Conrad still loved Selznick's art. The book was published in 1994. Selznick also drew pictures for Conrad's book *Our House*, which was published in 1995.

As a popular children's author and illustrator, Selznick is often asked to appear on television and give interviews.

ELEMENTS OF ART: LINE

Line is one of the most basic parts of art. Lines are used to define a form. They may contrast or repeat other lines. Selznick's illustrations use many lines! He creates them with pencils.

Pencils are usually made of charcoal or graphite. The marks of charcoal pencils can be smudged for shading. Artists can erase or smudge the markings of graphite pencils, too. But graphite is not as dusty. The graphite in drawing pencils also comes in a range of hardness levels. Each produces a different effect.

The next year, more work came Selznick's way. He painted the cover of Andrew Clements's book *Frindle*. And, he illustrated *The Meanest Doll in the World* by Ann M. Martin and Laura Godwin. Selznick's career was taking off!

EXPLORING HISTORY

Before long, Selznick began to work on **biographies**. He illustrated *Amelia and Eleanor Go for a Ride* by Pam Muñoz Ryan. It is about pilot Amelia Earhart and First Lady Eleanor Roosevelt's friendship. Selznick visited Washington DC to research the book. It came out in 1999 and became an **ALA Notable Children's Book**.

Selznick's next project with Ryan was published in 2002. *When Marian Sang* is about African-American singer Marian Anderson. She made history by performing at the Lincoln Memorial in Washington DC.

Also in 2002, Selznick's illustrations appeared in *The*

Dinosaurs of Waterhouse Hawkins by Barbara Kerley. In 1853, Hawkins introduced the world to dinosaurs by building the first models of them. Selznick flew to London, England, to see these dinosaurs and learn about Hawkins. Then he created the pictures for this fascinating book, which earned him a **Caldecott Honor**.

In 2004, Selznick visited poet Walt Whitman's childhood home in West Hills, New York. This prepared him to illustrate

Kerley's *Walt Whitman: Words for America*. That year, the book became an **ALA Notable Children's Book**.

These **biographies** were good stories about important people. And readers loved Selznick's illustrations. Yet he wondered if he would ever work on other types of projects again. His career felt stuck.

Hawkins's dinosaur models are still on display in Crystal Palace Park in London. Selznick spent time crawling around them to imagine how Hawkins felt creating them.

SOURCES OF INSPIRATION

For six months, Selznick stopped illustrating. Then, several events changed his life. First he met Maurice Sendak,

*A movie version of **Hugo Cabret** was filmed and released in 2011.*

author and illustrator of *Where the Wild Things Are*. Sendak told Selznick his art was good, but not yet his best. Selznick knew he was right. "Make the book you want to make," Sendak advised. His words meant a lot to Selznick.

Next, Selznick read *Edison's Eve: A Magical History of the Quest for Mechanical Life* by Gaby Wood. One chapter tells the history of **automatons**. Selznick became fascinated by them. Wood's book also discusses filmmaker Georges Méliès. Selznick learned that Méliès had owned numerous automatons. But sadly, they had been destroyed and thrown away.

In his head, Selznick suddenly saw a picture of a boy finding a broken automaton in the garbage. He knew this was an idea for a story. And he thought that reading it should be like watching a movie. Selznick's story would begin with the boy he had imagined, who would be called Hugo.

Selznick says the illustrations in Hugo's story are like "bursts of miniature silent movies."

Inventing Hugo Cabret

Selznick spent two and a half years working out the details of the rest of his new story. It takes place in 1931 in a train station in Paris, France. Hugo is an orphan who secretly lives there. When he finds a broken **automaton**, he wants to fix it. He believes it holds a message from his dead father. But an old man and a young girl complicate matters.

To research the story, Selznick visited Paris three times. There, he photographed streets and buildings. He also studied **mechanics**. Then, Selznick made detailed pencil drawings. These were much smaller than the final drawings in the book. In fact, he had to use a magnifying glass to see them!

Selznick's final drawings tell major parts of the story. In the novel, there are times when words disappear and pictures take over. As the reader turns the pages, the pictures change like images in a silent movie.

In 2007, *The Invention of Hugo Cabret* had a tremendous reception. The book remained on the *New York Times* best seller list for 42 weeks. It was translated into 29 languages. Best of all, it won the 2008 **Caldecott Medal**. This was the first time a novel had earned the award. Selznick had made history!

Hugo Cabret *is 533 pages long, with more than 300 pages of drawings. The book weighs almost three pounds (1.4 kg)!*

WONDERSTRUCK

Hugo Cabret was such a success that Selznick wanted to create another illustrated novel. For *Wonderstruck*, Selznick wove together two stories. Ben lives in 1977 and Rose lives in 1927. Selznick tells Ben's story in words. But he tells Rose's story through pictures. Many fans looked forward to the book's release in 2011.

Selznick is glad he found his true calling. In the end, his father's wish came true. His children all found jobs they love. Selznick's sister is a teacher, and his brother is a brain surgeon.

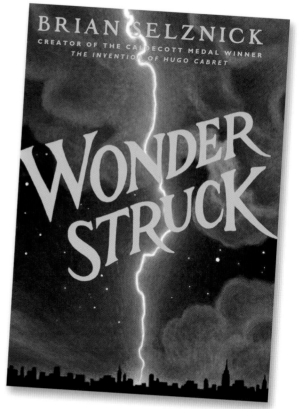

Tracy Mack, Selznick's editor at Scholastic, said, "How the two separate stories unfold and ultimately intertwine will surprise you."

Wonderstruck *features more than 460 pages of drawings!*

Today, Selznick spends his free time with his partner, David Serlin. They split their time between Brooklyn, New York, and San Diego, California.

Most likely, Selznick will continue illustrating more books by other authors. Readers also hope he will write and illustrate more books of his own. It takes time to write them, but he enjoys this work. After all, Selznick turned the things he loved most as a child into a wonderful career. Lucky for fans, it seems his career has just begun!

GLOSSARY

accountant - someone who records the amounts of money made and spent by a person or a business.

ALA Notable Children's Book - an annual award given by the American Library Association. Books are chosen for quality, style, and excellence.

archaeologist (ahr-kee-AH-luh-jihst) - one who studies the remains of people and activities from ancient times.

automaton (aw-TAH-muh-tuhn) - a machine that can move by itself, especially a robot.

biography - the story of a real person's life written by someone other than that person.

Caldecott Medal - an award the American Library Association gives to the artist who illustrated the year's best picture book. Runners-up are called Caldecott Honor Books.

manuscript - a handwritten or typed book or article not yet published.

mechanics - a science that is used to help design, construct, or operate machines and tools.

set - an artificial setting where a play is performed or a movie or television program is filmed.

WEB SITES

To learn more about Brian Selznick, visit ABDO Publishing Company online. Web sites about Brian Selznick are featured on our Book Links page. These links are routinely monitored and updated to provide the most current information available.

www.abdopublishing.com

INDEX